CATS ARE GOOD PETS

In Bloom ❀

By Cecilia Minden

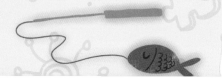

CHAPTER 1

Cats are good pets.

Cats like to run.

Cats like to run fast.

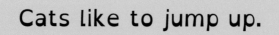

Cats like to jump up.

Cats like to jump
up on the bed.

Cats like to nap.

Cats like to nap on the bed.

Cats like to nap in the sun.

Cats like to nap in your lap.

CHAPTER 2

Cats like to hop.

It is fun to hop on a ball.

Cats like to sit on the step.

It is fun to sit on
the step in the sun.

Cats like to lick.

16

A cat likes to
lick his fur.

A cat likes to lick his paw.

A cat likes to lick your hand.

Cats are fun pets.

Cats are good pets.

WORD LIST

sight words

a	good	paw	your
A	like	the	
are	likes	to	

short a words
ball
cat
Cats
fast
lap
nap

short e words
bed
pets
step

short i words
his
in
lick
sit

short o words
hop
on

short u words
fun
fur
jump
run
sun